a positive version

volume one

pamela fields

S.H.E. PUBLISHING, LLC

A Positive Version
Copyright © 2021 by Pamela Fields.

All rights reserved. Printed in the United States of America. No part of this book may be used or reproduced in any manner whatsoever without written permission except in the case of brief quotations embodied in critical articles or reviews.

For information contact :
info@shepublishingllc.com
www.shepublishingllc.com

Book Cover and Title Page design by Michelle Phillips of
CHELLD3 3D VISUALIZATION AND DESIGN

ISBN :
978-1-953163-19-6 (paperback)
978-1-953163-24-0 (*She*Edition)

First Edition : October 2021

10 9 8 7 6 5 4 3 2 1

CONTENTS

1 | LITTLE CHILDREN

2 | A PRAYER IN MY POCKET

3 | AN EARTHQUAKE IN HEAVEN

4 | YOU TURN

5 | OH! MR. PREACHER MAN

6 | A FRIEND AND DECEIVER

7 | A MOTHER'S LUXURY

8 | WALKING IN THE COMPANY OF SPIRITS

9 | CHASING AFTER SHADOWS

10 | CHOCOLATE BLOOD

11 | CRIES OF THE CITY

12 | THANKFUL

13 | WHO AM I?

14 | TURTLE SOUP

15 | A DIALOGUE OF LOVE

16 | A RAW RELATIONSHIP

17 | YOU, SIR/MADAM!

18 | MESSENGER

19 | THE INVENTORY OF THE BLACK WOMAN'S SOUL:

20 | BLACK

21 | MARRIAGE ON THE ROCKS

22 | ACROSS A DEEP RIVER

23 | THE LONG JOURNEY HOME

24 | THE QUIET WARRIOR

25 | WHEN POVERTY CALLS

INTERMISSION

26 | WALK THE WALK, AND TALK THE TALK

27 | SOMEWHERE BETWINX

28 | FROM MY WINDOW PANE

29 | AFRICAN WOMEN IN AMERICA

30 | FACES

31 | REAL MEN'S TEARS

32 | ONE STEP ABOVE HELL

33 | EXPECTATIONS

34 | A SEA OF CLOUDS

35 | TAKE AWAY

36 | THE SPECIAL GIFT

37 | THE GIFT

38 | WHEN LOVE SUFFERS

39 | FRIENDSHIP

40 | ON THE OPPOSITE SIDE OF GIVING

41 | MY SOUL LONGETH

42 | SPRINGTIME PERSUASION

43 | THE BALL OF OPPORTUNITY

44 | THE DEATH ANGELS' PARADE

45 | A PRAYER REQUEST

46 | THIS HOUSE, IS NOT MY HOME

47 | I'M GOING HOME TODAY

48 | THE ANATOMY OF A HOME

49 | PLAN FOR SUCCESS

50 | REVERSE THE SCRIPT

ACKNOWLEDGMENTS

ABOUT THE AUTHOR

a positive version

volume one

pamela fields

1 | LITTLE CHILDREN

God gives mothers children
    To perfect her growth.

Answers to life's problems
    The wisdom to solve them,
        Are tested on you.

You are the product
    Of your mother's wisdom.

Tie your shoes,
    Make your bed,
        Eat your vegetables,
           Wipe your nose.

Look up straight,
    Pay attention,
        And count your blessings.

Your mother's instructions
    Multiplies into great rewards
        When you do the right thing.

2 | A PRAYER IN MY POCKET

WITH EVERY PRAYER That you bring to pass, there is one.

Like a parade marching, step by step
To a never-ending drummer's beat.
One by one do I count,
Every blessing as they manifest.
Yet, there is one.

Like candy in a candy store,
Gumdrops, Licorice, Peppermints,
Lollipops and Chocolates.
No! One will never do.
Because I've got a prayer in my pocket
Which says I can have the candy store.

Like a never-ending supply of dollar bills,
I can spend my prayer on whatever I please.

A POSITIVE VERSION

A prayer in my pocket to spend on what I choose:

A world of lost souls,
For every soul reclaimed by Salvation,
There is still one.

Sickness, illness and affliction
With every healing under the
Anointing power of the Holy Ghost,
There is one.

Hurt and deep seeded pain,
Outwardly displaying of hate and
Ultimate self-destructive acts,
There is hope, through the redemptive
Blood of Jesus Christ.

Yet there is one who have not heard the
Good News, nor have they seen.

So I think I'll pray, Dear Lord,
For the Miracles once wrought
Through the touch of the Master's Hand.

Miracles for all to see,
Testimonies of miracles for all to hear.

Miracles in the life of the blind,
The lame, the cast down,
Trodden over, forsaken and forgotten,
Lost children of God.

PAMELA FIELDS

It's not the magnitude of the prayer, But the depth.
Miracles birthing new testimonies
Every day, I pray.

3 | AN EARTHQUAKE IN HEAVEN

The blessings of the Lord
Are stored in heaven
With a bunch of other
    Good stuff.

God said he's going to cause
An Earthquake in Heaven
And Heaven is going to shake
    With a mighty quake.

The treasures are going to
Be loosen on earth.
The blessings are going to fall
    Like drops of rain from the sky.

A new commandment I gave unto you
That ye love one another, as I have loved you
That ye also love one another
    This commandment I left for a reason.

Like currency is used to purchase
Much gain and material wealth.
So shall those of you who have kept this commandment
    Soak in the blessings
    Which I shall loosen from the sky.

PAMELA FIELDS

An extra season added to the year
Winter, Spring, Summer, Fall.
Add to that the season of blessings
    Those who have kept
        My commandment will I bless.

Get ready for the Great Heaven Quake.

4 | YOU TURN

On a dark and lonely road,
Stretched endlessly ahead.
Brightly lit temptations winked
As oncoming traffic paraded
One by one each headed in a different way.

Directly ahead, flames of fire
Torched the way
Moving swiftly as I moved,
Red lights, tail lights, stop lights, go.

My thoughts were heavy,
A conscience slumber, the struggle was hypnotizing,
I dared not admit defeat,
The surrender at last was sweet toward sleep.

And in that moment of weakness,
When things it seemed were going great,
I took a wrong turn and
Ended in a ditch.

PAMELA FIELDS

Upon examination, I had no time to think,
Or wonder what to do,
Then I heard the angel whisper,
YOU TURN, quickly and get away.

That turn brought me up and out of that ditch,
With a leap, the wheels hit the pavement and
Went into a spin, flames of fire
Pointed the way, as I promptly
Accelerated and sped on.

No, no, no, there was no other vehicle
Hindrance on that road, the devil took an
Opportunity to lose upon me a spirit of slumber
With the intention to do harm to my life,
But God said no, and dispatched
Angels armed quick and ready.

My travels have not been quite the same
Since I heard the angel whisper
YOU TURN.

5 | OH! MR. PREACHER MAN

Oh! Mr. Preacher Man, from a sinner's point of view;
There's something you've got to tell me.
Well, there's something I got to tell you too.

You say you was like me until you found that man Jesus Christ?
But tell me how one man can save everybody's life?

How can He see all places at once?
And not come when there is danger?
Every devil knows, to the liquor bottle, I'm no stranger.

But Oh! Mr. Preacher Man, from a sinner's point of view;
How can you correct me, if you do the same things I do?

You drink on occasions, smoke weed and crack cocaine.
Then come out Sunday morning,
Telling us it's messing up our brain.

So you ain't did it in a while, you say He healed you from that.
But if you ask me Mr. Preacher Man,
I don't see why you'd wanna be healed from crack,
And as a matter of fact,

If you ask my opinion,
Give me a wine bottle, you'll see my decision.

See, if you ask me, you got a couple of new suits,
A nice house and things,

PAMELA FIELDS

But Oh! Mr. Preacher Man, remember,
how long you say you been clean?

How you gonna preach to us about Jesus Christs,
I don't see no Jesus helping me out in my everyday life.

So until I meet this Jesus, I'm not trying to believe.
And that Holy stuff you say God gave you,
I'm not trying to receive.

So Oh! Mr. Preacher Man, from a sinner's point to view;
If this Jesus you're talking about can save you,
Can He save me too?

By: Nikia Fields

6 | A FRIEND AND DECEIVER

They call him a friend, but
    His real name is SIN.

He says, disobey your parents,
    And hang out with me.

He says, they don't want you to have fun,
    Don't want you to be free.

He says don't go to school,
    It's just for fools.

Who need to learn or
    Obey those stupid rules.

My friend wants me to hang
    And smoke a little weed.

Sell drugs, make quick money,
    They say, that's the way to succeed.

He says steal what you want,
    You don't have to pay.

PAMELA FIELDS

But your friend never tells you
    The cost is your life.

So resist the Devil,
    And he will flee.

Find a friend name Jesus,
    And have true victory.

He won't lead you wrong,
    Because His way is right.

For your other friend is
    A theft and a liar, he wants to take your life.

For Jesus gave his life for you
    That you through Him would know
        There is no greater friend than Jesus
            Anywhere you go.

    By: Angelina Cooks

7 | A MOTHER'S LUXURY

A hot bath with bubbles;

Dishwashing liquid, squirt just enough

Under running water, that'll do.

A fresh perm;

A trip to the hairdressers

Ah, makes me feel like queen for a day.

PAMELA FIELDS

A safe recreation;

A family outing;

And no out of pocket expense,

Wow, let's make this a date.

An extra hour of sleep;

Tack it on anywhere during the day;

Add it to the morning, an afternoon nap,

Or maybe retire early in the evening;

Sleeping beauty never had it this good.

Moments of meditation;

Snatched during the course of a day.

Perhaps a cup of fresh coffee, or a glass of ice

Tea, a good book, a relaxing chair;

All add to the pleasure of this moment.

A POSITIVE VERSION

An adult conversation;

Not gossip, not lecture,

But straight talk from the heart.

Being free to speak of your opinions drawn

From your own personal experiences.

Wild Flowers

Gathered in the hands of your youngest.

Presented to you,

Roots, clogs of dirt and all.

Dinner's a breeze,

When there's plenty of what we had yesterday,

Just waiting to be warmed.

PAMELA FIELDS

Chocolates, a slice of cake,

Particularly homemade,

And if I didn't have to do the baking myself.

A cool breeze of air,

Blowing in our direction,

On an unusually hot summer day.

Where are the children?

Why is it so quite in here?

They're gone to visit their aunt,

Or a dear relative for a day or two.

Great laughter, small laughter

Any tickle spell at all.

A POSITIVE VERSION

Expressions of love,

Speaking louder than words,

Shown in caring, and in deeds,

Sweeping the floor,

Washing the dishes,

Cleaning the rooms,

Without being told, it's as good as gold.

8 | WALKING IN THE COMPANY OF SPIRITS

Scripture say that we entertain
Angels unaware.

Spiritual promotion lifts the conscience
    And elevates it to the knowledge | or knowing |
        Of the spiritual world.

The presence of angels is in the air:

God's anointed power accompanies us
in everything we do.
Taking the form of the Holy Ghost,
being invisible to the naked eyes.
Yet the power from it moves,
and the evidence of it revealed.
With the tongue do we make our confession.
With the heart we believe.
Faith being the element that moves God.

Spiritual wickedness moves in and
out of our presence all the time.

Its demonstration hinders a man or
a woman from being righteous.
When it moves in our children,
it causes rebellion.
Tricking them to sin and unrighteousness.
Being of spirit, no one sees its traps.

A POSITIVE VERSION

But when you're walking in the company of Spirits.

Whisper a command, or shout it
At the top of your lungs.

That wicked spirit has to acknowledge
    The authority of the Spirit of God
        Standing tall inside you.

9 | CHASING AFTER SHADOWS

When the whisper of a hope
    Is so real,

Anticipation kicks in and
    The chase is on,

Looking for the hope of
    The manifestation.

Like the widow woman and the lost
    Mite, she searched.

Searching in dark places
    Under the shadows.

Shadows, in search of a manifestation.
    The chase, is so real, only to reveal nothing.

But the hope is still there
    Which means undying faith;
        Unwavering faith.

Seeking those things that be not
    As if you're chasing after shadows
        Until they come to pass.

10

CHOCOLATE BLOOD

I confined in you, that I was pregnant, again.

Confined in you as I did because I was afraid.

Afraid that I wasn't sure which man I had slept with,
was the father.

Afraid that the cocaine that flowed through my system,
would in some way harm that child.

Out of panic and fear,
I turned to the people I knew I could trust.

And this is what you said to me:

> Destroy the Black Child
> Abortion, was it the only way?
> Chocolate blood spilled,
> Never to be reclaimed.

People whom I trusted, who so many times in the past,
many thoughts of wisdom you've shared with me.

As I sit and ponder, deep behind the cell chambers of my mind,
locked away and throw away the key.

PAMELA FIELDS

An internal prison,
forever locked in the prison of my innermost thoughts.

Thoughts of the plot, and the motive,
a scheme of destruction. But oh, this is not the end.

A crime of passion,
and the evidence blows in the wind saying, Mama, Mama:

> Destroy the Black Child
> Abortion, was it the only way?
> Chocolate blood spilled
> Never to be reclaimed.

Repentance I seek, for the guilt at my own hands.

No one to blame, no shame will I claim.

A permanent mistake, to scar the heart.
Not a tear shed, not even the blues.

But in the wee hours, and if you're true, "I remember"
thoughts and "I wonder if" thoughts come in like a flood.

Haunted thoughts of what could have been:

> Destroy the Black Child
> Abortion, is it the only way?
> Chocolate blood spilled
> Never to be reclaimed.

11 | CRIES OF THE CITY

I have heard the cries for help, and
I have seen the signs of desolation.

How long will this great nation continue to put off what is
obviously the weak link in a great chain? Don't you hear?

They're saying, "How much longer must we wait?
I can't hold out, can't hold on any longer."

We have our Nike shoes, and our designer clothes.

Our supermarket shelves are filled with
a wide variety of every kind of food.

Buildings and skyscrapers are going up all around us.
And the late model cars are driven in our streets both near and far.

Fast food restaurants stretch clear across the country,
selling everything from breakfast, lunch, to dessert, and in every
culture do they exist.

Our airplanes, trains, and
buses travel to every city on the map.

This is a day of high tech and the year of the computer.

PAMELA FIELDS

The year of automation, plastic money,
rapid refunds, fax it, direct deposit.

In the winds do I hear a starving people crying for help.
"When will I be heard?

When will my flight be known?"

Atomic bombs that fight our wars,
but the wars of the inner city are left unheard.

Where are our leaders, our teachers, our preachers,
and our government officials?

Who cares, who will take the time to care?

We say we don't know the cries; don't care to know;
don't care even when known.

I have heard the cries.

In greed do we wake up and in selfishness do we lie down.

The progress of some is the doom of others.

Come and listen with me,
let us hear together what cries are heard.

It is the cries of the Black Man's future, our youth is crying:
"I'm down, I've been wounded, my sky seems so high.

In desperation do I try to mend my link to that great chain that
reaches up so high.

Who will see me and who will hear?

Poverty has heard and my cry is weakened.

A POSITIVE VERSION

Illiteracy has heard and has spread to produce and reproduce, now doubt has taken over and yet I cry.

Sickness and disease have heard my cries and although they're choking me, I cry out.

The waste of the world is upon my shoulders. Tobacco and alcohol have heard my cries, for they are so close, they are so near, they are everywhere.

Hear my cries, oh great chain and know my flight.

Hear me, hear me, for I'm weak.
I have been wounded and I am down.

Dope and drugs, they're listening to me right now.

My sky which seems so high, has turned a darkened gray.

12 | THANKFUL

GOD MADE TREES; NOT WEEDS.

PRAYERS OF FAITH BEGINNING AS SEEDS.

SUPPLY AND MULTIPLY ALL OUR NEEDS.

OPEN YOUR EYES, AND RECOGNIZE!

SEEDS OF LIFE, PLANTED ON GOOD GROUND.

FERTILIZED WITH LOVE THAT ABOUND

ALL AROUND.

THROUGHOUT THE YEARS,

WATERED WITH MOTHER'S TEARS.

FROM THE DEEP, APPEARS,

FRUIT BEARING TREES.

13 | WHO AM I?

I AM LIGHT PIERCING THROUGH A DARK, DARK WORLD.
A distant star, a ray of light.
I am hope.

I AM GREETINGS THAT MAKE YOUR DAY.
Hello, good-bye, Please and Thank you.
Inspiring and uplifting greetings.
I am love.

I AM SUNRISE; ANOTHER DAY; OPENING UP;
Beginning with; starting first with the sunrise.
I am new.

I AM SHADOWS, BLACK SHAPES MOVING IN THE NIGHT.
Shapes that go boo, and hide themselves just beyond
The sight. Silent shadows.
I am fear.

I AM TIME, TICKING AWAY AND RUNNING OUT;
Like the hour glass and the sun dial.
The sun hanging low in the sky. Tic, toc, tic,
Spent time. I am old.

I AM LIFE, BEGINNING WITH A SEED,
Fertilized within an egg. Growing, struggling from stage to stage
To reach the canal. Thus, being born into life.
I am one. I am alone.

PAMELA FIELDS

I AM A BIRD IN A TREE. WATCHING, SINGING, CHIRPING,
Beautiful bird.
I am tall.

I AM LEAF FALLING SOFTLY. RED, ORANGE, YELLOW
Leaf falling.
I am soft.
I am beautiful.

I AM RAIN DROPS; WET AND COLD AGAINST YOUR NOSE;
That makes you smile. Little rain drops.
I am joy.

I AM A COTTON TAIL HOPPING, LEAPING, JUMPING,
Skipping, Bouncing; gentle cotton tail.
I am up.
I am down.

I AM

The End.

12 | TURTLE SOUP

Turtles on the side of the road;

Frogs in the yard.

Snakes in the outhouse;

Alligators in the lake;

And Fish in the pond.

15 | A DIALOGUE OF LOVE

Eye language

Smile language

Need language

16 | A RAW RELATIONSHIP

When you hurt,
I hurt.
When you dance,
I dance.
When you're warm,
I'm warm.
When you're cold,
I'm cold.

17 | YOU, SIR/MADAM!

Must you smell like a walking death?
Must you walk around
Smelling like the casket that
Will one day engulf you?

An invisible killer
You willingly invite.
At your own hands,
Do you struggle?
No, you do not.

Now there's a message,
Which lingers
And it spells D-E-A-T-H.
And death smells!

One more puff,
Puff, puff, puff,
The invisible killer
Has invaded;
And now has accessibility
To destroy you.

18 | MESSENGER

Messenger From Hell,
    Your Love Is Like a Cheap
        DRUG.

And although I Crave And
    Ache For It; This Is One
        Pain That I Must Bear.

Although I Look for It at Night
    And Am Ruled by It in My Dreams,
        Touch Me Not, Less I Tell.

Memories Of the Lovers That We Once Were
    Send Thrills of Hope
        To Chill My Spine.

Keeper Of My Heart, Let Me Go!
    Cause My Mind Is Free,
        But My Hand to Another, I Wed.

19 | THE INVENTORY OF THE BLACK WOMAN'S SOUL:

The Wealth of the Black Woman,
Lie in the clutches of her mind.
Her success and power are
Her strong will and determination.

The struggles of yesterday
Keeps her in focus with the goals of tomorrow.
Reflections of a sea view of todays,
Make her purposes a realistic challenge:

Teen pregnancy and gang banging youth
Presenting a special problem in her world.
It robs them of their God given freedom
To step out in this world and to
Express creativity, individuality,
Unity and peace.

This Black Woman comes with gifts
In every smile, and in every conversation.
Listen to the messages from the wealth,
Spoken from the mind of the Black Woman.

A POSITIVE VERSION

The tears of the Black Woman
May express sadden memories locked in the heart.
Memories that only time must heal.

No doctor of medicine and no,
Not even prescription drugs
Will make the tears cease
From strolling down her face and
Dripping off her chin.

No alcoholic beverages can doust the pain.
No marijuana joint, pill popping, or
Dope smoking caravan can remove the sting.

But time has prescribed its own remedy.
And in time, understanding with
Some laughter should produce enough joy to
Ease and heal the sadden tears of the heart.

Now there is a flip side.
Tears of joy, reflect happy memories
Creating an aura all aglow
From the smile on her face.

Hands of a Black Woman
Are designed with a very special purpose.
Because with those hands,
A Black Woman expresses much love.

Hands which tuck her babies in bed at night,
Are the same hands which scold
Them in their mischief.

Hands which prepare her family's meals.
Dishpan hands carefully removes and cleans,
Then dries and tuck away the evidence.
Ties, laces and buckles up shoes.
Then untie and ties them back again when needed.

PAMELA FIELDS

Healing hands that soothe hurt,
Bandages wounds and dries tears.
The hands of a Black Woman
Instructs, and protects, gives direction,
Prepares treats, wipe away tears,
Warns and points, strokes, caresses,
Massages and prays.

With every touch of the hand of a Black Woman,
Much joy is shared.

The Black Woman's hair;
Short, long or curly.
Glorious in all her array;
Black, red or gray.

There's a parade on board every city's bus when the
Black Woman struts her stuff.

Lift up your head Black African Queen
With a Little African Pride,
Gentle Treatment or Soft Sheen;
Crème of Nature, "S" Curl or Ultra Sheen.

A bun, a tuck, a roll;
Braids, and waves that go dip.
Cuts in shags, layers and feathers.
African styles, naturals and head wraps.
Ponies and phonies only your hair
Dresser knows for sure.

A Black Woman's Beauty
Is in her smile
It's in her hair
It's in the way she walks
It's in the way she talks

A black Woman's Beauty
Is in the way she sings

A POSITIVE VERSION

It's in her hands and her feet
It's in the twinkle of her eyes
In the roundness of her backside
And the curves of her hips.

A Black Woman's Beauty
Is in her laughter
It's in her special touch
It's in her deeds of good-will.

When a Black Woman is robbed of her outer beauty,
Her inner beauty is greatly seen
Through the test of time.

The Children of the Black Woman
Are precious jewels of the River's Nile.
Reviled beneath the sands deep
Within the river's floor.

The jewels of the River's Nile
Hidden treasures of talents,
Gifts of treasures,
Sparkling and shinning,
Riches and wealth,
Lurking to be found.

Deep in the heart of the Nile
Lie a wealth, waiting.
Pay close attention to the secrets of this silent Nile,
Which flows in the same direction.

Wealth untold, precious and rare.
Solid gold lies in the minds of
Children of the Black Woman.

20 | BLACK

BLACK is me,
BLACK like the dark shadow,
BLACK like the womb;
My mother's womb from which I came.

I close my eyes, and
BLACK is all I see, then I find peace.
BLACK like the midnight,
All is quiet, all is still.

BLACK against white paper
It is printed on.
Release thoughts from within my
BLACK soul.

BLACK pepper
BLACK out
BLACK eyed peas
Mary Matt, dressed in
BLACK

BLACK on BLACK crime, replaced by
BLACK ON BLACK love.

When I close my eyes,
BLACK is all I see,
In the wee hours of the
BLACK night;
I pray and meditate within my
BLACK soul;
Please Lord,
Help this BLACK, BLACK world.

21 | MARRIAGE ON THE ROCKS

For Better, or For Worst
In Sickness, or In Health
For Richer, or For Poorer
Til Death We Do Part.

I now pronounce you man and wife. Vested time.
Vows of sincere pledge. A pledge between me and my betroth.
Witnessed in the company of friends and loved ones.
A mental handcuff.
A life sentence, close the doors, throw away the keys.
Partners for life, one for all and all for one.

My associates may say to me, because I've been off the scene,
"Where have you been?"
The only honest reply I could give is that I've been sick.
Not a physical sickness where your body parts, whether internal
Or external, hurt so bad that it causes you to lie down,
Medicate, or seek the help of a physician.
A sickness of the mind, an invisible cause, no pain and no ache.
My mind caught a virus because I chose "For Better or For Worst,
Til Death We Do Part.
Vows spoken in love sent the two
Cruising toward life's sweet highway.

PAMELA FIELDS

Pitfalls and snakes and crocodiles.
You watch my back and I'll watch your back.
Cruising and steering afloat a lifetime journey.

But what are you cruising in? And what happens when it wrecks?
Or through the Test of time, it wears out?
Now what are you floating in?
Mess and a sea full of trouble.

The pitfalls, snakes and crocodiles are all around.
You can't watch anyone's back
Because you're too busy watching your own back.

Your life long partner has gone and cut a deal with the enemy.
Now you're sleeping with the enemy who want to contaminate your
mind and cause you to fall.

I'm sick, I tell you. An invisible germ led to a virus in my mind.
Now only the test of will can save me.

My will…is to be free from this mental handcuff.
My will…is for this cruise to end and
Start again in different directions.

22 | ACROSS A DEEP RIVER

When I started this walk,
There was a vast, deep river before me.

When I knew anything,
I woke up and the river was behind me.

And I heard the voice of God say,
"Go back, and bring others across."

Now I understand and my calling is sure.
I'm here for one reason and one reason only.
One mission, one people, called by God
Bind together, like glue, by the Love of God.

That love being made perfect in us is unconditional.
Drawing the sinners by the very demonstration of God's love
Are yokes broken.

Now the river currents were strong,
I saw in there a soul reaching out for help.
Struggling desperately against the currents.

As the soul went down for a second time
I knew that I couldn't just stand there and watch and do nothing.
I couldn't think about how deep, nor how strong the currents.

I knew that God had entrusted this soul in my hands.
I needed to reach this soul,
And Love sent me diving into the deep.

23 | THE LONG JOURNEY HOME:

What obstacle keeps me from returning? What force or wall,
what partition would continue to separate me from my birthright?

Hope winks at me, like a shadow
desperately do I chase after.
Love points my direction and love,
pure and shameless do I chase after.

The birthright was given.
The system took it away one cold winter day. From that time forward the storms won't go away.
Now I seek the long journey home.

Constant conversation to the Father.
Help me to see the way,
let the right things be done in me I pray.

I'm not lost, nor am I purposely rude. I'm a young child and I need my mother, no other.

A POSITIVE VERSION

*Somewhere within this big great city,
lies a merciful Judge who will
unlock the door.*

*Within the city limits, a bomb awaits to be sprung.
Simply Because no one admits... the wall that separates
my mother and me has a balance symbol and 'In God We
Trust'
which is why so much grief.*

*I long for your arms, dear mother, and the safe journey
onward, toward home.*

24 | THE QUIET WARRIOR

Finding a lost soul in a dry and weary land,
is a treasure to God. Finding lost souls is a
special job assigned to that willing warrior.

The job requires cleaning and washing lost souls one by one, like a bucket of filthy chitterlings.

Gleaning lost souls that are cast down and trodden over, forsaken and troubled, complex and possessed.

Finding lost souls for God
In answer to prayers of weeping mothers.

Finding lost souls for Christ
In the Kingdom building business.

Finding lost souls
In the gutter of their bondage.

Souls weary of the spirit of addiction, the spirit of lust,
Homelessness and despair,
deep seeded depressions and demons of hate.

Finding lost souls as a soldier on the front line,
an anointed, quiet warrior,
armored in the work of the Lord.

A POSITIVE VERSION

Finding lost souls in battle,
Pulling off in order to pull down.
Fasting, praying, reading God's word with a focus.

Binding spiritual wickedness in high places.
Interceding in the secret places of the Most-High,
Focusing on that need that is tearing families apart.

Mighty in action, through the power of God Almighty,
Meeting the needs of people in performance.
Deeds of good works toward men.

Working in the vineyard of God's footstool,
Along the highways, byways and hedges,
Interceding, never ceasing intercession.

Searching high and search low,
Meeting quotas against the mighty
Number in which God has called.

God's anointed, quiet warrior exhibiting the light of Christ
through a smile, kindness and good deeds,
With love, patience, and all the fruits of the spirit.

Fighting God's way, armored with the
ammunition of God's anointed words.

Faithfully ministering the seed of hope,
In an hour such as this.
Turning on the flash light of my soul
Searching for lost souls in dry places.

25 | WHEN POVERTY CALLS

WHEN POVERTY CALLS,
HANG UP QUICK,
WRONG NUMBER,
IDENTIFICATION UNKNOWN.

 WHEN IT COMES KNOCKING AT THE DOOR,
 QUICK, SHUT THE DOOR,
 AN INVADER IS SEEKING ENTRANCE,
 AN INTRUDER, ACCESSIBLITY ONLY BY YOU.

AND IF BY MISHAP THAT INVADER GETS IN, THIS YOU'LL SEE, HE'LL WEAR HIS WELCOME OUT:

A BARE CUPBOARD.

A BARE REFRIGERATOR, ICE TRAYS AND COLD WATER IS WHAT IT HAS TO OFFER.

A PILE OF DIRTY LAUNDRY THAT'S SAYING,
"WASH ME, WASH ME."

A POSITIVE VERSION

I BARELY HAVE ENOUGH,
MAYBE I CAN WASH A FEW.
A LITTLE BIT OF WASHING POWDER,
NO DISH WASHING LIQUID AT ALL.

A LITTLE COMET, A LITTLE BLEACH,
SOME HOW I'LL MAKE THIS HOUSE SPARKLE.

WHEN POVERTY COMES A KNOCKING, BRACE YOURSELF
AND COUNT IT ALL JOY. GOD SEES YOU AND HE CAN
ANSWER PRAYERS.

WHEN THAT FINICKY CHILD SAYS, "MAMA, I'M HUNGRY,"
AND THERE IS NOT A HOT DOG NO WHERE TO BE FOUND.

WHEN THE BILLS ARE DUE, GAS AND LIGHT AND THE NOTE
TOO. THE PHONE IS DISCONNECTED, AN EXPENSE LONG
OVERDUE.

THE SINK IS BROKE, THE CEILING IS BROKE TOO AND NOW
LEAKS. WHAT WILL I DO? IN THE ONE BED-ROOM
APARTMENT SITTING IN THE REAR?

SOMEONE TAKE THE COUCH TONIGHT, SOMEONE TAKE THE
COT, AND SOMEONE TAKE THE FLOOR.

NO CARFARE, NO CARFARE AT ALL, I'LL HAVE TO WALK,
YES, THAT'S WHAT I'LL DO.

MANY HARD TIMES COME AND MANY WILL GO, BUT

PAMELA FIELDS

POVERTY COMES AND MOVES RIGHT IN. THE BIBLE SAYS AND I QUOTE, "I NEVER SAW THE RIGHTEOUS FORSAKEN, NOR HIS SEED BEGGING BREAD."

THE CONSCIOUS OF THE RIGHTEOUS WILL BELIEVE GOD, BUT ALL TOO OFTEN THE VOICE OF ANOTHER CAN BE HEARD, AND WILL MOVE UPON YOU IN LIGHT OF YOUR CIRCUMSTANCES AND WILL LEAD YOU TO CRIME.

WOMAN, DON'T SELL YOUR BODY.

MAN, DON'T ROB THAT OLD LADY.

THERE IS A HIGHER POWER AND
THIS IS YOUR TEST.

YOUNG PEOPLE, DON'T SELL THOSE DRUGS.
FOR WHEN YOU DO, YOU CURSE YOURSELF.
YOU CURSE YOUR HOUSEHOLD, AND YOUR PEOPLE.
YOU'RE SETTING YOURSELF UP FOR A LONG HARD ROAD,
YOU'LL SET YOURSELF UP A WINDING ROAD, A NEVER-ENDING ROAD, AND ONCE YOU HAVE SET YOUR COURSE ON THIS ROAD, IT'S HARD TO GET BACK, AND YOU'LL MEET DEATH, AT THE WRONG END OF THE ROAD.

BUT BECAUSE POVERTY IS NOT GOING TO STAY UNLESS IT CAN TAKE OVER, HERE IS WHAT YOU DO.

COUNT YOUR BLESSINGS,
MY HEALTH IS FINE,
AND MY FAMILY IS TOGETHER.

A POSITIVE VERSION

PRAY AND READ YOUR BIBLE AND
KNOW THAT GOD IS IN CONTROL.

AND WHEN YOU HEARKEN UNTO A KNOCK AT THE DOOR.
AND IT'S YOUR NEIGHBOR, SISTER OR BROTHER OR WHOM
EVER, YOU KNOW, THE ONE WHO USED TO CALL YOU ALL
THE TIME AND ALWAYS ASKING YOU, "WHAT YOU'RE
COOKING TONIGHT." YOU TELL THEM, "THERE'S NO FOOD."
AND SEE DON'T GOD MAKE THEM A BLESSING UNTO YOU.

A POSITIVE VERSION
una versión positive
INTERMISSION

A POSITIVE VERSION
o una versione positiva
INTERMISSION

26 | WALK THE WALK, AND TALK THE TALK

After living a Christian life and walking with Christ for many years, my life reflects holiness in every thing I do and say.

The Oil of Salvation has anointed me to walk through trials, with many heavy blows, thrown in my direction.

The weight of which,
    The heaviness,
        And mental anguish of it all,
            Had to come under subjection.

The pain,
    The hard times,
        The hurt,
            And the tears,
                All these I had to bear.

PAMELA FIELDS

Now I have grown, I am mature in the Lord.
   I see hope, when there was once none.

With everything that I've gone through,
   I've learned perseverance,
      I've learned tolerance,
         I've learned true joy,
            And temperance to endure hardness,
         Yet the strength to keep right on marching.

Well, I've stopped crying now
   have accepted to take the challenge,
      And I will survive.

27 | SOMEWHERE BETWINX

Twilight's owl
And first rays of morning's dawn.

Sleepless nights, I toss and turn
Trying hard to find a land of
Dreams, where I could set my
Visions and get lost during that time
Somewhere betwinx
> *Twilight's owl*
> *And first rays of morning's dawn.*

In between winks, amist sounds within
The night that goes
creak, crack, tic, toc, drip, drop;
My lover's arms of comfort and strength
I long for near, and he me
Somewhere betwinx
> *Twilight's owl*
> *And first rays of morning's dawn.*

PAMELA FIELDS

And when sleep has abandoned me,
My lover's arms, it seems are so far from me;

I bow down in my secret place:

Dear Lord,
    Show me your beautiful mercy again
    This day I pray
    Somewhere betwinx
        Twilight's owl
        And first rays of morning's dawn.

28 | FROM MY WINDOW PANE

Thick plastic plexiglas window panes, just me.

Glimpse of times past:
snowflakes falling on a cold winter's day
hustle and bustle of the people passing
clothes wrap tight, mittens, hats and scarves
children playing, in the snow
tracking wintertime snow into my house
raking leaves, mowing the lawn, springtime rain
falling gently against my window pane
hopscotch, jump rope, bat-n-ball, and jacks
birds chirping, busy little squirrels, dogs barking,
chase the cat and make'm run
cars cruising down my street
stop light, yellow light, go
these scenes epic pictures I observed upon close
examination with much regard.

Behold today, what scenes I view:
headline news
Oklahoma bombing,
train crash, plane explosion in mid air

PAMELA FIELDS

girl X, raped and left for dead
racial crimes, of deep seeded hate
O.J.'s ex's lying in a pool of blood
war on rap, shoot to kill
scandal in the white house,
violence in the streets, gun smoke in the air
hunger and starvation, the homeless is everywhere
preacher caught holding the pistol
survey these sights, witnessed for all to see,
what an aspect.

Visions of tomorrows:
blue skies and rainbows,
open your mouth preacherman and preach the word
brotherhood like never before,
peace and harmony everywhere
neighbors loving neighbors, all in the hood
family unity, respect and appreciation
children learning values, morality and self-respect
A day where hunger is no more
babies protected from grown up affairs
warfare, abortion, and of course prejudice must go
drugs and gang war activities, vanished like a ghost
senseless murders, crimes of passion, hate crimes ceased
look at the appearance that these spectacles show,
a brighter outlook, with closer inspection what prospects.

29 | AFRICAN WOMEN IN AMERICA

It's hard to be an African Women
    In America.

When the Brother that you sleep with ain't
    Really your Brother.

It's hard to be an African Women
    In America.

Because the Brothers all look the
    Same, their skin just like mine.

It's hard to be an African Woman
    In America, and a Sister too.

Economic status is the game
    That the Americans play.

Sisters got game, they got the moves,
    Listen to the status quo.

PAMELA FIELDS

And it goes something like this:

> *My bed, my money, my honey*
> *Cost of living, on the rise*
> *Brother got a sweep rap,*
> *Cause his honey got some money,*
> *Carrying on the grooves,*
> *Ding, dong, the Brother made it to the bed,*
> *Now he got some honey.*
> *Brother in my bed,*
> *Trying to take over my game.*

Brothers in America, they got to go!
>   Go and get some game.

Sisters ain't Sisters if they ain't got game,
>   Cause Sisters got too much…
>   Intellect and independence…
>   They play the game to win.

Get out of my bed Brother
The honey is getting bitter.
You don't have to be an American,
>   But be an African.
Stop trying to play my game
And get your own game.
You don't have to be an American
>   But be an African, Brother.

30 | FACES

As I march to the tune of the Christian parade,
I never turned back.
I marched in tune to every beat,
In step with every other saint.

We the Christians march in this world.
But we are not a part of this evil and wicked place.

Then I stopped along the way.
To observe quite another face,
Full of hurt and despair, troubled and anguished.

Something within me reached out.
That same thing within me understood.
Could it be that I remembered?

How could I continue, when there was such a need?
Could I truly be blessed, if I continue to pretend,
I don't care? I don't dare.

How could we who are not of the world
Forget to show God's love?
Speaking with the tongues of angels;

PAMELA FIELDS

Having the gift of prophecy and understand mysteries;
Bestowing goods to feed the poor;
And faith to move mountains.

Serving in the Church kitchen,
And really don't want to be there
Fussing along the way at all these greedy Saints
And even more so, at all these wasteful Christians.

Singing in the Choir,
Rocking to the beat of the Christian rhythm.
Finger popping, and swaying from side to side,
What we all need to be, is on one accord.

Teaching Sunday School, a few of these
Lessons need to get down in the Teacher's soul.
To understand the truly importance of
Being a disciple of the Lord, and delivering the Word.

Truly, there is other ways to show God's Love.
Wings tarnished with the smoke, and filthy language
As I turned aside to notice the faces of the real world.
For this purpose, to earn stars in a heavenly crown.

The church as we know it today
Began so many years ago.
The whole story is told in the Book of Acts,
With the spreading of God's Word,
And the teaching of the Gospel.

A POSITIVE VERSION

However, there was something much, much more
That was evident in that day:
Faith in God and in His Son, Jesus;
Hope in the return of Christ one day, and
Charity (Love), shared among the brotherhood.
Of the three, Love being the greatest.
For God is Love.

As I stopped along the way of my Christian march
I stopped to notice, and
Once more to study the faces of the world.
I have been studying that these faces are not bad,
But that many have been hurt.
In the process of the many who have been hurt,
Go on to hurt others and to hurt themselves as well.
And the cycle goes on and on.

The Christian march,
Many are too busy to notice.
Otherwise, insensitive to the faces.

Outer scars, of cigarettes,
Drugs and alcohol;
Which hide the deeper wounds of hurt,
Are all that they see.

Is there any balm in Gilead?

31 | REAL MEN'S TEARS

An emotion that every human being understands.
Tears are an expression from the deepest
> Part of a man's cravings.

And not unlike any other emotion.
Love, joy, pain, anger, fear, sadness, and sorrow;
> Tears must be expressed.

When we look back at the deepest part of our history;
The story as we understand it is such, that tears is not
> Always something that men like to do.

But the true history of the Black Man was birth from the
tears shedded when they lost their freedom.

Jewelry of chains and shackles;
Tears are like a treasure locked and stored away.
> Redeemed only when the need arises.

A POSITIVE VERSION

The Black Man reached down within and found that they had to release the bountiful treasure to express the sorrow of leaving the motherland.

Just like a baby, cut from his mother's womb;
Only to experience his own emotions.

Many have said that it's the whack across his rear,
With his heels upward, but the pain that he must experience is his own.

His mother's womb, no longer a protective haven.

Emotions have to be expressed. If not, they build up and causes anger, or worse he is numb; without feelings, without expression, without emotions, good or bad, just numb.

Emotions are being sensitive to feelings that upraise within you. Real Black Men learn to have control over the most powerful treasure that there is, the treasure within.

It distinguishes the difference between strong and weak
And it exercises its strength by allowing that power to be expressed.

Weak men are not weak because they show emotions.
They are not weak because of their tears. They are weak because they do not exercise the power of control.

Thus, allowing their emotions, their tears,
Their inward feelings, to control them.

It's like a game of cards, you let the opposing team Player
see your hand. Or a game of football, your
Strategy revealed before it's time.

Thus, the opposite team is ready for all your moves.
In life, one can believe that there is a time for every
emotion, whether it be:

LOVE, the supreme emotion, shown through kindness,
respect, gratitude, appreciation and honesty. LOVE is an
expression that is shown between lovers, but differs in
degree when shown to parents and family. However, there
is yet a different LOVE shown among brotherhood and to
self. A supreme LOVE shown to the maker of mankind.

JOY, is yet another emotion which is shown with much
happiness, a smile, laughter, cheers, a shout, clapping and
dance.

Both of these emotions may produce tears. Tears of Joy;
Tears of Laughter; Tears of a Glad Heart; All to be
expressed.

Sorrow, grief and sadness produce quite a different Kind of
tears. It is the pain that a person feels which cannot be
expressed in any other way. Hurt that will not go away or

A POSITIVE VERSION

reverse itself. It taunts and hunts you. It pries at your heart and pierces. Hurt or pain must be expressed or it will eat you up from the inside. It will tear you down and cause you to hurt others, to be hurt yourself and to abuse.

Let the tears flow my brother.
Let the tears flow my lover.
    Let the tears flow my father.
    Let the tears come forth my sons everywhere.

You have an abundance of them.
You are rich and enriched by them.
    You are distinguished by them.
    You are made strong by them.

It is your birthright, given to you by a nature.

32 | ONE
STEP
ABOVE
HELL

ouldn't you know it, hell's doors and its gates are left wide open.

The flames from it are like unto a bar-b-que pit where the charcoals are manned and well kept, nice and hot.

The sizzle of souls scorched under the blasting heat can be heard, the smoke is blinding, causing a cough in the throat and leaving a stench,

One | Step | Above | Hell.

It's no fair, it seems that someone keeps pushing.
Pushing back across the threshold of temptation.
That someone, something is none other than the devil.
Because God tempts no man.

A POSITIVE VERSION

Caught up somewhere in the stages
Of my mind is a state of weakness.
Knowing like I do, but caught just the same,

One | Step | Above | Hell.

It's busy here, a many have trodden in this place.
Some even predict their own destiny, and I quote,
"I'm going to the big party there's going to be in hell."
Laughing and joking, eating, drinking and making merry;
Getting drunk off strong drink and high off popping and smoking and shooting up.

They fail to realize that the party they refer to is right here,

One | Step | Above | Hell.

I close my eyes, and I see that there is higher ground.
In order to obtain it, I've got to want it.
How can I focus on that place when the bondage of
Sin has got me shackled, ball and chain?
When I would do better,
The curse of temptation places me under arrest.
Misery and depression keep company with me,
This is not a lonely place.
Misery loves company and depression is its side kick.
Who will rescue me, from a Quicksand of sinking,

One | Step | Above | Hell.

The gospel is told, in the land of hallelujahs and amen;
About the Saviour's miraculous birth
His message to the people, that God lives and
His triumphed death,

PAMELA FIELDS

Which paid the price and paved the way to
Victorious living right here in the dressing room
Of life am I on stage.

The message told by Matthew, Mark, Luke and John
About the Saviour, Jesus.
Jesus is the answer, He will rescue you.
You have a right if you're….

One | Step | Above | Hell.

Call, Jesus.

33

EXPECTATIONS

If I could sow a seed today,
Within the souls of man:

That seed would be HOPE.

Not HOPE as in "Maybe,"
But HOPE as in "I Believe."

If I could fertilize that seed today,
That's in the souls of man:

That fertilizer would be FOCUS.

FOCUS as in never letting go.
Focus as in not wavering between two points.
FOCUS as in the upper most on your mind.

If I could water that seed today,
That's in the souls of man:

I would water that seed with PATIENCE.

PATIENCE fortified with strength to endure.
PATIENCE demonstrated with courage.
PATIENCE, as in calmness.

PAMELA FIELDS

If I could, I would watch that seed grow today
In the souls of man.

I would watch that seed grow,
In the souls of my people.

I would watch that seed grow
Prayerfully, until it grows
Expectedly into a beautiful blossom.

34 | A SEA OF CLOUDS

Lost in the sea of storm clouds,
On every turn, dark rolling, tempest storms.

Fiery trials of faith, lonely dark midnight hours.
Sinking sand on every hand.

God is so faithful to fight every one of your battles:

> To the storm, He says, Peace be still.
> To the fiery trials, He'll bring you out pure as gold.
> In the midnight hour, He is the star of hope.

Because the sun must shine,
He'll hide you in a secret place.

He'll keep you in your darkest hour
Lest you should happen to fall.

He asks just one thing,
That we hold on to His Hand, and not let go.

35 | TAKE AWAY

You can take away my finances,
You can take away my job,
You can take away my income,

You can take away this earthly roof,
You can take away this earthly shelter,
You can take away this building of stone.

You can take away my love ones,
You can take away by separation,
You can take away by pulling us apart.

But you can't make me doubt Jesus.
You can't take away my will.

The word of God still lives in my heart.
And you can't take away my joy.

36 | THE SPECIAL GIFT

My Mother birthed me
    Into this world.

My Father provided
    The seed.

The Lord God Almighty
    Gave me life.

The Enemy, the Adversary, the Devil,
    Gave me a good whipping growing up.

But the greatest gift of all, a very special gift,
Was the new birth into salvation, through Baptism.

The redemptive power of God's love,
    His healing power,
        And the power to put the Devil in his place.

That very special gift,
    Is the Gift of the Holy Ghost.

37 | THE GIFT

Every morning that I wake,
There is a big package tied with a red bow.
I am the package, and the red bow is
The sanctified blood running through my veins.

My Saviour, my Lord gives it to me
With all of his love, no strings attached.
And, it's free, saying here is your life again today,
I'm giving you this day.

Then I open my eyes and behold,
The package is so big, I walk right in.
And everything that I'll need for the day,
My Lord is so thoughtful to include.

Food, shelter and protection,
Joy is in the package.
Peace, it's in there
Prosperity in faith, also included.

My gift to Him,
I will use his gift.
Showing kindness to everyone I meet.
Helping the lost and showing them in.

Reaching out, and out reaching to the needy.
Telling them how much He cares,
And before I lay my head to sleep,
I'll say, Thank you Lord.

38 | WHEN LOVE SUFFERS

I really do hate it when you hurt.

Your pain is so real, and with all your strength do you bare.
        The disfiguration of your face,
As you fight to hold back all too willing a release of tears.
        Or to release expressions that sound like you're in pain.

Then I focus as I watch you lying upon your bed;
        A well deserving rest and longing for peace.
Our Lord and Saviour Jesus,
        As He held the lamb precious and near.
Gave me to know that upon your bed,
        Is where you needed to be.

And I thought once again,
        And gained contentment to know;
That the disfiguration of the face,
        Showing of outwardly pain,
Is far better than the disfiguration of the heart,
        In trying to cope with the inward pain,
                Of a contrite spirit and a broken heart.

I knew that the pain was real on both,
        Outwardly and inward pain.
Made me to think on the lowly Jesus.
        A crucifixion of outwardly pain,
                Our Lord and Saviour as He hung on the cross.

PAMELA FIELDS

Disfigured, a Lamb, both precious and dear,
    A longing for peace and well-deserved rest.
But the disfiguration of our Saviour's heart,
      Meant more to us when He cried, Abba Father,
          Forgive them for they know not what they do.

39 | FRIENDSHIP

friend in a ship is carried, toss and blown to and fro
their path driven toward the same destination
will have to be friends till the end
you may ask me why I say this
because of the vast ocean in which their lives float
keep them from seeking another

friend in a ship is free and pure
take a favor, take a body to talk to,
take a shoulder to lean on, to cry on,
take a loan, take a helping hand,
take, take, take, take till it hurts,
then take some more
take time, take attention, take concern
take understanding and compassion,
why not, it's free, friend

friend in a ship, it's the one thing that is still free in the world
one might say, why do you let it be, why do you let it go on like that,
then I might say that the only reason tis so is because of
the friend in a ship, why where else could I be
if my friend in a ship and I were not,
what would be left is an empty ship

so I ask, which is the friend and which the empty ship
the one placing job, money --- the love of it or the lack
the other placing the only thing above friend in a ship is
matrimony, salvation and the
call to motherhood.

40 | ON THE OPPOSITE SIDE OF GIVING

On the outskirts of a city,

    Across a little pond,

        Where the ducks and geese

            Gather in the spring time.

In a little house,

    Across from a field,

        Where the grass grows greener

            And the flowers bloom early.

There in that house lives a family,

    Who honors and reverence the Lord?

        Every Sunday the family would go

            And give praise and thanks to the Lord.

A POSITIVE VERSION

The family would give their tithes and offerings.

    Where ever they went,

        They were sure to give an encouraging word,

           A smile, or tip of the hat.

It seems that the family learned the golden rule a long time ago,

    To give of themselves over unto the Lord.

        So they gave their hands

           Over the ministry of helps.

Their mind they gave to learning more about the Lord.

    They gave their knees to bending in prayer.

        They gave their soul to a people,

           A lost generation.

Their eyes they gave to weep bitter tears.

    Their feet they gave to walking throughout the city,

        Carrying good deeds as they go.

PAMELA FIELDS

They gave their time as a dedication to service.

    Their mouths, they gave to speaking God's word,

        And telling people of the Gospel of Christ.

      But their hearts,

          They gave wholly to God.

And God gave back, for you see

    The family lived in the little house,

      And the head had not worked in years.

But the provisions of God is sure

    Because He knows what things we have need of.

      No good thing will He withhold

      From them who love Him.

And so the Lord blessed this family.

    You see, the opposite side of giving,

      Is to be blessed, you can't beat God giving.

41 | MY SOUL LONGETH

I'm praying for the God giving power to literally
    Snatch souls from the grips of the Devil,
        Unbeknown souls, who are unaware
            That the Devil is out to get them.

I'm afraid to ask for anything more,
    At this time, I've learned to have patience.
        But Father, do we have the time to spare?

The demon of drugs and alcohol,
    Coupled with the demon of homosexuality,
        Where so many have fallen,
            Is a web of confusion.
                A tactic, a ploy used by the
                      Devil and his angels.

I need help Dear Lord.
    How can I continue to sit still,
        And allow this ruthless enemy
            To kill and steal what is not his?

PAMELA FIELDS

My soul longeth for the answer to this generational problem
    An answer which can only come from you.

When the menace has attacked like a cancer.
    A Disease, cankerous and contagious.
        My soul longeth for the cure.
            The secret ingredient of surety,
                Might I find in thee.

O, pray my soul, in all earnestly.
    Pray a way will be made.

O, seeketh my soul's sake,
    At what awaits.

In a desperate hour,
    When hope it seems is lost.
        Quivers my spine
            As it weeps in awe.

O awaken upon me,
    Let it dawn in my spirit,
        As we run this race.

Your mercy and grace
    Is given without measure.

O press upon me for all to see,
    Your forgiving nature, O God.

42 | SPRINGTIME PERSUASION

**GENTLE BREEZES OF
SPRINGTIME PERSUASION.**
Loose the over coat of wintertime scenes.

Springtime persuasion produces smiles
And laughter arouses the springtime air.

**SPRINGTIME BRINGS A GENTLE
PERSUASION THAT MAKES**
The dogs leap, bark, and chase with pure joy.

Springtime persuasion's sheer joy
In the hearts of little boys, it makes them hop and jump.

**SPRINGTIME PERSUASION
IS IN THE AIR,**
Rain drop rain, wash away the earth tones
of wintertime scenes.

BLOW AWAY, WINTERTIME, BLOW AWAY
With the soft breezes of springtime persuasion.

43 | THE BALL OF OPPORTUNITY

Life is comparable to a baseball game.
Everyone has their chance up to bat.

As the batter prepares and gets in batting position.
The ball of opportunity is pitched his way,
As the ball approaches,
The batter swings with everything he has.

STRIKE ONE:
Teen Pregnancy, unwed mothers;
Mama's baby, Papa's maybe
Fathers being call to child support court.

STRIKE TWO:
Drugs and alcohol;
Pill popping:
Marijuana smoking;
Shooting up Heroine;
Ready rock, Crack, Cocaine;
Narcotics; is the name of this game,
Dope ain't no joke.

Wine, booze, intoxicating drink;
Moonshine and spirits that will blow your mind.

A POSITIVE VERSION

STRIKE THREE:
A Life of crime;
Gang Banging, Dope Pushing;
Killing and stealing.
Standing before the judge;
The offenses are stacked;
Doing time in the county jail.

NEXT BATTER:
The ball of opportunity is pitched his way.
It's a hit,
A fouled ball.
The ball of opportunity was hit.
This player finished school, landed a job,
And was to take a running start in the game of life.
But crack cocaine prevented the gain.
A fouled ball,
A pop up, the ball was caught.
And this player is out.
Next time up to bat; he'll foul again, and again, and again.
He'll foul until he gets it right.
Crack cocaine and life don't mix.

NEXT BATTER:
The ball of opportunity is pitched.
He takes a swing and hit the ball,

And is off to first base.
This player makes it to first base;
And is in the game of life.
A good education started him off in the right direction.

PAMELA FIELDS

If he stays in the game,
He'll go on to second base and land a good job.

One more hit and on to third base, you're on your way.
Why not start a family and mold a life?
For your child will be truly blessed;
With all the good attributes you have to give.

The next hit, a grand slam.
This player must have prayed before coming to bat.
A hit with power and the Holy Ghost.
And as the players make it to the home plate;
This game is not over,
Cause now we get to play the game in a successful way.

The rule of this game is somewhat different.
The objective of the rule is to keep the ball.
Touch down, Tackle, Kick Field Goal;
You have the ball; will you keep it?
Dribble, Dodge and Pass;
Two points, Free Point,
The ball is in your court.
Team Play, Strategy and lots of Prayer.
You have the ball; will you keep it?

44 | THE DEATH ANGELS' PARADE

AN ARMY OF DEATH ANGELS ARE BEING RAISED.

EACH IS GIVEN INSTRUCTION TO GO AND BRING BACK A LIFE. NO ONE SEES HIM AND NO ONE HEARS HIM, THE DEATH ANGEL COMES AND THEN GOES.

SOME WILL GO TO HOSPITALS AND SMOTE THE LIFE OUT OF THE SICK. SOME WILL BE GIVEN A SPECIAL ASSIGNMENT BECAUSE OF THE APPOINTED TIME IN SOMEONE'S LIFE HAS COME. AND THE BIOLOGICAL TIME CLOCK HAS COME TO THE LAST HOUR.

SOME WILL PREY ON NEW BORN BABIES AND BABIES STILL IN THE WOMB OF THEIR MOTHERS. GOD HAS A SPECIAL PLACE IN HEAVEN FOR THESE BABIES.

THEN YOU'RE HAVE SOME AGGRESSIVE ANGELS. THEIR APPROACH IS BY MEANS OF DANGER.

A WOMEN WALKING DOWN A DARK STREET, SNATCHED AND KILLED. A CAR ACCIDENT, WHERE THE DRIVER WAS NOT CAREFUL AND SPED ON AND MET WITH A COLLISION.

PAMELA FIELDS

A GROUP OF YOUTH WALKING HOME FROM SCHOOL. WHEN SUDDENLY DRIVE BYS; GUN SHOTS AND GUN SMOKE IS IN THE AIR. THE SCREAMS AND CRIES OF THE YOUTHS EVERYWHERE AS THE VICTIM LIES DEAD WITH THE PUDDLE OF LIFE GUSHING OUT OF THE WOUND.

SOMEBODY, CALL AN AMBULANCE, BUT IT'S TOO LATE.

DEATH ANGELS ARE IN THE AIR. DEATH ANGELS ARE EVERYWHERE. DEATH ANGELS WITH DIVINE PERMISSION AND THE ONLY AUTHORITY GIVEN TO TAKE A LIFE.

THIS PARTICULAR ARMY HAS ALMOST COMPLETED THEIR TASK. EACH ONE, ONE BY ONE COMPLETES THE MISSION AND RETURN TO THE MISSION GIVER. AND EVENTUALLY ALL BUT ONE HAS RETURNED. THIS ANGEL'S PREY IS ON A CHILD, A SCHOOL AGED CHILD, PREFERABLY UNDER 12 YEARS OF AGE. HIS APETITE HUNGERS FOR THE TENDER BLOOD OF A CHILD.

MOTHERS ARE YOUR CHILDREN COVERED UNDER THE BLOOD? CHILDREN, ARE YOU SAVED, PERCHANCE THE DEATH ANGEL MEETS WITH YOU? ARE YOU SAVED?

DEATH ANGELS ARE RIDING TONIGHT.

45 | A PRAYER REQUEST

My Prayer today and everyday
is that the Lord would give me <u>WORDS</u>.

Words of encouragement.
Words to uplift and to soothe the sorrowful heart.

Persuasive words to the sinner man
that would make him change his mind.

Words of wisdom
to the youth and foolish hearted.

From Genesis to Revelations,
the Holy Bible is full of words.

Soothing words,
audacious words, words of great men of old.

Give me words Lord.

Words to motivate, and to stir the soul.
Words that make a difference.

PAMELA FIELDS

Words to speak peace in the life of men and women.
In their homes, in their families, their neighborhoods,
communities and jobs.

Words that's loaded.
Words of truth. Words of strength.

A constant supply of words,
written and spoken.

Words of meaning,
Living words courageous and sure.

Words to instruct.
Words that express.

Words to bridge gaps.
Caring words revealing love and joy.

Words from the heart,
sincere and loving.

Polite and kind words
never running out.

Words to speak God's authority
when the threat of the enemy's presence is near.

Words are going to the battle field.
Anointed words, shielded and shall not come back void.

Words that will not be defeated. Words spoken with a purpose.
Like an arrow soaring till it find its target.

46 | THIS HOUSE, IS NOT MY HOME

My house is this earthly flesh
Every spot, every bruise, every ache.

My Home is at Heaven's Gate.
Its address is Up Heaven's Road
Somewhere on High.

Pain visits my earthly house sometimes,
And it makes me want to cry.

But when I get Home,
No more pain and no more crying there will be.

My earthly house gets tired sometimes,
So I think I'll sleep now children.

Just remember the directions to my Home.
It's the straight and narrow way.

Dust off your dusty road map, the B-I-B-L-E.
And come see me when you too
This earthly house shall shed.

PAMELA FIELDS

**So when you think of me,
Remember that mama is at Home.**

**Oh what joy there'll be
When we meet again at
Haven's Gate.**

47 | I'M GOING HOME TODAY

WHEN THE GREAT Freedom Train Rolled Up,
All Aglow from The Saints on Board,
Singing A Heavenly Song
And A shouting Could Be Heard.

WHEN THE KNOCK Came at The Door,
The Angel with Invitation in Hand,
(Calling Her by Her New Name)
Saying_____, We Are Waiting for You, Are You Ready?

I CAN SEE Mother Now,
With Ticket in Hand,
Took Only a Moment to Reflect,
Won't They All Be So Happy,
I'm Going Home Today.

WON'T THEY ALL Be So Happy.

NO MORE PAIN,
NO More Hurt,
NO more Bills and Money Problems,
I'm Going to A Better Place, I'm Going Home.

PAMELA FIELDS

NO MORE MISUNDERSTANDING,
Or Being Misunderstood,
NO MORE HILLS to Climb,
NO More Crying,
I'm Going to A Better Place, I'm Going Home.

Our Mother
A New Name,
A New Shout,
A New Song,
A New Robe,
And A New Home, She Has.

ONE DAY, IF WE LIVE RIGHT,
Heaven Will Be Our Home Too.
But for Now, Let's Rejoice, Mother Is at Home.

48 | THE ANATOMY OF A HOME

WHO WOULD KNOW BY
looking at this humble bathroom,
That it is kept swept and clean.
Like my own hair, I would neatly brush and pin.
But if it were a grand hair style
adorned with combs and curls;
Not unlike the bathroom, adorned with lace and pearls.
Everything tucked and, in its place,
just one look and all would know.

The kitchen is like the reproductive organs.
The key is to use it to produce joy and such delights.

The bedroom is like the stomach.
Because there are needs that must be fed with a little wink.

The living room is like the feet.
When it's (an eye) sore, it makes a statement
to the mood of the housekeeper.

The halls are like the arms of the body extending.

PAMELA FIELDS

And the several places it leads to is like the hand, reaching.
Reaching that area or destination that you intended.

The dining room is like the buttocks, backside, or seat.
A comfortable spot used just for sitting.

The basement is like the mind of the house.
With the network of its structure all in delicate detail.

The staircase is like the legs of the body.
Seldom wanted to be exercised.

The dust in the house is like the skin,
That you must polish and oil.

The windows are the eyes of the house.
If they're open, and the lids are up,
we'll know you're awake and at home.

The aromas of the house are as the nose of the body.
Fragrance, scent, musty, odor just a whiff.

The greetings of the house are as the mouth of the body.
Hello, Good Bye, Please, and Thank You;
all makes this a very pleasant stay.

The backbone of the house is its financial status.
But the heart of the house is that family.

49 | PLANS FOR SUCCESS

Plans for success starts first with a seed.

    A seed,
             A vision,
                      A hope,
                              A desire,
                                      A prayer.

A seed to nourish.

A vision for focus.

A hope for all.

A desire of the heart for prosperity.

A prayer for power.

                    Put it all together

                    Plant it, water it daily

                    And mix well with Faith.

50 | REVERSE THE SCRIPT

The big play writer came to town. He had an interesting proposition for a grand play he wanted to Sponsor.

It would be so easy. During this African American season, he would present the play using a brilliant cast.

His brilliant plan was to present history as it has been. He wanted to include slaves, slave owners, task masters, a couple of run-a-ways, a rape scene and of course a scene where a family member is being sold off to another slave owner, separated.

The day came for auditions to begin, and scripts to be distributed. When all Had assembled, he looked at the White Man, and said, "You will be the slaves." And this Black Man over here will be playing the part of a slave owner. "I've written the play," he said excitedly where he will rape your daughters and assign Task masters to you to make sure you work from sun up to sun down. Oh yea, this Black Man right here will be playing the role of the mean old whipping boy to tear meat off your back using his whip.

So the scripts were assigned and read. To much of a surprise, the Black men assigned to those roles would not take the roles and respectfully bailed out. It seemed that portraying the roles of history in the reverse explained one, "was morally wrong" so wrong in fact that he declared he could not and would not do, even in acting that same wrong thing that was done to his ancestors.

Moral of the story, it was wrong then and it is wrong now, and two wrongs do not make a right.

A POSITIVE VERSION

ACKNOWLEDGMENTS

First and foremost, I'd like to thank God for allowing me to go through my journey of life in which I have been able to learn and grow from my circumstances, and change my challenges into this beautiful work of art and book series of poems.

And to my mother, Leola Reynolds, whom told the best stories when I was growing up. My love for her and her stories as she told us as we were growing up were quite splendid.

And to my readers, I am grateful for your support I'd like to offer some wisdom. When an older person has a story to tell, sit down and listen because it will be a good story, one of true wisdom.

ABOUT THE AUTHOR

Born to Gentle Frank Fields and Leola Reynolds, Pamela Fields grew up on the south side of Chicago, Illinois, where she attended several elementary schools and Wendell Phillips High School, all schools located in Chicago, Illinois. She also attended Harold Washington Junior College and would go on to major is Early Childhood Education. She later attended Prestige Nurse Aide Training Academy, where she attained her certification as a CNA. Both of the selected majors were encouraged by her experiences of not wanting any child to be left behind, nor any older adult left uncared for.

Fields held the position of being the oldest of her siblings, one sister, and two brothers. She refers to her brothers and sister as stair-steps as each sibling is one year apart from the other. Fields acknowledge her siblings and Richard Reynolds, her superhero and second husband to her mother, for preparing her to understand and learn several tactics of dealing with the way of the world. Fields has three children: Nikia Fields, Edward Fields, and Shana Edwards, and she loves them all dearly. Her children have blessed her with eight grandchildren, and Fields continues to shower them with the educational packages from her homemade learning lessons.

PAMELA FIELDS

Getting into the professional side of life, Fields was employed at several early learning centers. She also worked as a CNA on weekends, and she spent a few evening hours taking care of her mother. Her years of employment with others have led her to her Happily Ever After, becoming a future best-selling author with S.H.E. PUBLISHING LLC, and starting up two businesses simultaneously, one being K.I.N.D.N.E.S.S. Kare (*Keys IN Developing & Navigating Effective Social Solutions*), a childcare service, and Pam's Baking Handz.

Ultimately, Fields purpose and passion is to bring together ordinary people like you and me with the commitment to encourage us to love one another. She believes that it's the small efforts of a friendly smile, the gift of gratitude, praying for one another, and small acts of kindness that will change the world one day, one hour, and one second at a time. It only takes a second to yield a smile and patience doesn't cost anything.

Thanks for reading!
Please add a short review on
Amazon and S.H.E. PUBLISHING LLC.
Let me know your thoughts!

www.ingramcontent.com/pod-product-compliance
Lightning Source LLC
Chambersburg PA
CBHW011406070526
44577CB00003B/394